The New York Times

POCKET
MBA
SERIES

S0-BIU-502

MANAGING INVESTMENT

25 KEYS TO PROFITABLE CAPITAL INVESTMENT

ROBERT TAGGART, PH.D.

Boston College

Lebhar-Friedman Books

NEW YORK • CHICAGO • LOS ANGELES • LONDON • PARIS • TOKYO

For *The New York Times*
Mike Levitas, Editorial Director, Book Development
Tom Redburn, General Series Editor
Brent Bowers, Series Editor
James Schembari, Series Editor

Lebhar-Friedman Books
425 Park Avenue
New York, NY 10022

Published by Lebhar-Friedman Books
Lebhar-Friedman Books is a company of Lebhar-Friedman Inc.

Printed in the United States of America

Library of Congress Cataloging-in-Publication Data
Taggart, Robert, 1945–
         Managing investment : 25 keys to profitable capital investment
/ Robert Taggart.
         p.   cm.—(The New York Times pocket MBA series ; vol. 9)
      Includes index.
      ISBN 0-86730-778-1 (pbk.)
      1. Investments.   I. Title.   II. Series.
      HG4521 .T25   1999
      333.6—dc21   99-27694
                                                               CIP

DESIGN & PRODUCTION BY MILLER WILLIAMS DESIGN ASSOCIATES

Visit our Web site at lfbooks.com

INTRODUCTION

LEBHAR-FRIEDMAN BOOKS is proud to present *The New York Times* Pocket MBA Series, 12 invaluable reference volumes that are easily accessible to all businesspersons, from first level managers to the executive suite. The books are written by Ph.D.s who teach in the MBA programs in some of the finest schools in the country. A team of business editors from *The New York Times*— Mike Levitas, Tom Redburn, Brent Bowers, and James Schembari—provided their own expertise to edit a reference series that is beyond compare.

The New York Times Pocket MBA Series offers quick-reference key points learned in top MBA programs. The 25-key structure of each volume presents an unparalleled synopsis of crucial principles of specific areas of business expertise. The unique approach to this series packages academic books for consumers in an easy-to-use trade format that is ideal for the individual businessperson as well as an excellent training reference manual. Be sure to get all 12 titles in the series to complete your own MBA education.

Joseph Mills
Senior Managing Editor
Lebhar-Friedman Books

25 KEYS TO PROFITABLE CAPITAL INVESTMENT

CONTENTS

KEY 1

Sound strategy +
Timely investment =
Shareholder value

I t is one of the most basic premises in business: the primary objective of corporate investment is to create value for shareholders.

Spending on projects such as new plant, equipment, and research and development affects a company's business prospects years into the future. And because a company's share price reflects investors' best estimates of future cash flows, those expenditures, which can reduce operating costs, enhance product quality, or otherwise build a company's competitive advantage, should result in a higher share price.

Focusing on shareholder value does not imply that others with interests in the company, including creditors, suppliers, customers, employees and the local community, are unimportant. Any company acting consistently against the interests of its other stakeholders will harm its business prospects and ultimately destroy shareholder value. Nevertheless, shareholders are the

Money was never a big motivation for me, except as a way to keep score. The real excitement is playing the game.

Donald Trump, Trump: The Art of the Deal

company's owners, and they will judge managers' performance by the yardstick of equity market value.

Critics charge that focusing on shareholder value forces managers to overemphasize quarterly earnings to the detriment of long-term prospects. However, numerous studies have shown that share prices tend to rise after a company announces new capital spending and R.&D. programs, suggesting that the stock market will recognize and reward such efforts.

But a company can't be careless. Capital spending programs that create shareholder value are the products of carefully crafted business strategies. Companies such as Coca-Cola, General Electric, Merck and Procter & Gamble, which have been steadily successful in creating shareholder value, all have clear strategies for building and maintaining competitive advantage. Investment spending that is not well thought out and not driven by a sound business strategy can destroy shareholder wealth. Several studies have found that share prices fall if the market perceives that a new strategy or an acquisition blurs a company's focus by moving it into unrelated businesses where it has no competitive advantage.

For example, AT&T tried to move into computer manufacturing in the mid-1980s. After several years of losses the company increased its commitment to computers by acquiring NCR for $7.5 billion in 1991. However, investors reacted negatively and AT&T's total stock market value lost an estimated $4–$6 billion as a result of the transaction. In contrast, when the company left the computer manufacturing business in 1995, the company's stock market value rose 10.6 percent, or more than $9 billion, on the day the restructuring was announced.

A good business strategy identifies sources of potential advantage over competing firms. If a firm can build barriers to entry, it can exclude competitors from encroaching on its business or at least gain a head start. Pharmaceutical firms like Merck use patent protection in this way. Other sources of competitive advantage include economies of scale and scope. If average production costs decline with the scale of operations, a company that achieves large-scale operations before its competitors can establish itself as the market's low-cost producer. Similarly, a company like Procter & Gamble that expands to include many related products can achieve economies in marketing and distribution compared to single-product competitors.

Regardless of their source, any company strategy that builds competitive advantages is likely to require a steady stream of capital expenditures. However, if investors are convinced of the soundness of the company's strategy, these expenditures will be reflected in a higher stock price.

KEY 2

Cash flow counts

W hile a sound strategy can affect a company's stock, what investors really look for is cash flow. An investment project's ability to generate cash flow determines its potential for creating shareholder value.

However, cash flow and accounting profit are not the same. Net income recognizes revenues and expenses when goods are shipped to customers. However, the company has not yet received cash if customers buy on credit. Similarly, if a company buys supplies on credit, the time at which expenses are incurred precedes the time at which it pays suppliers in cash.

Money has a time value. Thus, shareholders are more concerned with cash flowing in or out than they are with income statements. Shareholders ultimately derive value from corporate ownership through current or anticipated cash distributions.

The yearly cash flow measure that is relevant for corporate investment analysis is:

Net Cash Flow = Revenue − Operating expense − Taxes +
Depreciation − Increases in net working capital −
Gross capital expenditures

Net cash flow differs from net income in several ways. First, operating expense, but not interest expense, is deducted from revenue. Interest expense is reflected in the discount rate. Because interest expense is excluded from the cash flow measure, the tax calculation is not the same as in the income statement. Rather, we calculate taxes by multiplying the company's effective tax rate by operating income (the difference between revenue and operating expense).

Depreciation is added to the cash flow measure because it is a noncash charge. Depreciation does have cash consequences, because it is tax deductible. That is why it is deducted from revenue before calculating the project's tax bill. However, the depreciation charge has not been spent in cash, so it must be added back after taxes have been calculated.

Subtracting increases in net working capital (current assets minus current liabilities) from cash flow adjusts for differences between income and cash flow. For example, if a sale is booked, but not yet collected in cash, accounts receivable must increase by the amount of the sale. Subtracting the increase in accounts receivable thus adjusts for the fact that the sale has not yet generated any cash. Similar adjustments result from subtracting increases in inventory or adding increases in accounts payable.

Finally, gross capital expenditures must be subtracted. Many projects require further cash investments during their lives, and this is a cash outflow for the firm.

To illustrate, suppose a project has sales of $1 million, operating expense of $600,000 (which includes $100,000 in depreciation), and interest expense of $50,000 in a given year. The company faces a tax rate of 35 percent. During the year, cash balances devoted to the project, accounts receivable and inventory increase by $10,000, $20,000 and $30,000, respectively. Accounts payable increase by $25,000, and the company spends $400,000 on project-related equipment.

Net income for this project is $(1,000,000 - 600,000 - 50,000)(1 - 0.35) = \$227,500$. However, project cash flow for the year is $(1,000,000 - 600,000)(1 - 0.35) + 100,000 - (10,000 + 20,000 + 30,000 - 25,000) - 400,000 = -\$75,000$. Although the project has positive net income for the year, it has a net cash outflow, because of the additional expenditures for working capital and equipment.

KEY 3

A dollar today is worth more than a dollar tomorrow

I n addition to its size, the timing of cash flow is important in determining project value. Cash can always be invested to earn a return. Therefore, cash received now is more valuable than cash received in the future, because cash received now can be invested for a longer time. This principle is known as the "time value of money."

Suppose I can earn 5 percent per year on money that I invest, and I am saving toward expenses that I expect to incur in 10 years. If I receive $1,000 now, invest it immediately and keep on reinvesting all interest, I will have $1,000(1.05)^{10}$, or $1,628.89, at the end of 10 years. However, if I receive $1,000 eight years from now and invest it at that point, I will have only $1,000(1.05)^2$, or $1,102.50, 10 years from now. Thus, $1,000 received now is worth more than the same sum received eight years from now.

How much is $1,000 received eight years from now worth today? The answer is $1,000/(1.05)^8$, or $676.84, because if I invested $676.84 today, I would have $676.84(1.05)^8 = $1,000$ in eight years. We arrived at the figure $676.84 by "discounting" the future $1,000 back to the present. The assumed 5 percent return is the "discount rate," and $676.84 is the "present value" of $1,000 to be received eight years from now.

To value the stream of cash flow from an investment project, we first estimate the return we could have earned by investing in another, similar risk project. Using this as our discount rate, we then calculate the present value of each of the expected future cash flows and add them.

To illustrate, suppose an investment is expected to generate cash flow one, two and three years from now of $5,000, $10,000, and $7,000, respectively. At a 5 percent discount rate, the present value, P.V., of this stream is:

$$PV = \frac{5,000}{1.05} + \frac{10,000}{(1.05)^2} + \frac{7,000}{(1.05)^3} = 19,879.06$$

We will have numerous occasions to use this discounted cash flow, or D.C.F., technique. It is also helpful to have two formulas that cover special cases. The first is a perpetual annuity, or an investment that generates identical annual cash flow forever. If the annual cash flow is C, and the discount rate is r, the present value is:

$$PV = \frac{C}{r}$$

For example, the present value of a perpetual stream of $100 per year at a 5 percent discount rate is 100 divided by .05, or $2,000.

A variation is a "growing perpetuity," in which the

annual cash flow stream starts at the level C_1, but then grows at a constant rate g per year. In this case, the present value is:

$$PV = \frac{C_1}{r - g}$$

For example, if the cash flow starts at $100 in the first year, but grows at the rate of 3 percent per year, the present value, at a 5 percent discount rate, is $5,000.

We will find it useful to know these special cases when we estimate the terminal value of an investment. This is the value that we believe the project would have at the end of the analysis period.

KEY 4

Follow the net present value rule

The simplest types of projects require an initial investment in exchange for a stream of future benefits. If I buy an oven for my bakery business, its price is the initial outlay. The stream of future benefits consists of the yearly cash receipts from selling the cookies and bread that I bake in the oven minus cash operating expenses, such as the cost of flour and sugar, wages and rent. A natural measure of the oven's net benefit is the sum of the present values of all inflows and outflows of cash that are expected over its useful life. This is the oven's net present value (N.P.V.).

For example, suppose the oven costs $20,000 and is expected to generate a net cash inflow (receipts minus cash expenses) of $8,000 per year for each of the next four years. If the appropriate discount rate is, say, 10 percent, the oven's N.P.V. is:

$$NPV = 20,000 + \frac{8,000}{1.10} + \frac{8,000}{1.10^2} + \frac{8,000}{1.10^3} + \frac{8,000}{1.10^4} = \$5,358.9$$

N.P.V. is a summary measure of an investment's costs and benefits. Because all future cash flow is discounted, we can add its present values to arrive at the amount we would be willing to accept today in exchange for the oven's future benefits. N.P.V. also nets costs against benefits. That is, cash outflow has a negative sign, while cash inflow has a positive sign. Thus, if N.P.V. is positive, the project has a net benefit and is a worthwhile investment.

A positive N.P.V. also signifies that a project's market value exceeds its book value. For the oven project, initial book value is the cost, or $20,000. Under competitive bidding, however, bakers would be willing to bid as much as the present value of the oven's benefits to secure its services. At that price, the oven would be exactly a borderline investment. Thus, interpreting this hypothetical bid price as a market value, the oven's positive N.P.V. indicates that its market value exceeds its book value.

Other measures of investment value are sometimes used, but they are inferior to N.P.V. Some companies stipulate that any investment must pay for itself (i.e., cumulative cash inflow must exceed the investment's cost within a certain period, say two years). However, such a rule would exclude projects like the oven, which does not pay for itself in two years yet still has a positive net benefit. Companies also use a project's accounting rate of return, defined as average earnings before interest but after taxes, divided by the asset's average book value. However, accounting income doesn't necessarily reflect cash flow (see Key 2), and book value can be distorted by depreciation, which doesn't necessarily reflect the rate of decline in market value over the asset's life.

One other measure of investment value is the

Internal Rate of Return (I.R.R.), defined as the discount rate that equates the present value of a project's future benefits to its initial cost. For the oven project, for example, we can solve for the I.R.R. as 21.86 percent. Because this exceeds the project's discount rate, the I.R.R. rule calls for undertaking the project. In general, projects whose I.R.R.s exceed their discount rate have positive N.P.V.s. It is not true, however, that if one project has a higher I.R.R. than another it also has a higher N.P.V. Thus, N.P.V. is the best overall criterion for both deciding whether a project is worthwhile and for ranking projects in order of desirability.

In the long run men hit only what they aim at.

Henry David Thoreau

KEY 5

N.P.V. = Incremental Shareholder Wealth

A major advantage of relying on the N.P.V. criterion for investment decisions is the direct relationship in an efficient capital market between positive net present values and increases in shareholder wealth. The following example illustrates this relationship.

Suppose a company has assets that are expected to generate operating cash flows of $100 per year forever. If the appropriate discount rate is 10 percent, the discounted cash flow value of the assets, using the perpetual annuity formula from Key 3, is 100/.10, or $1,000. The company is entirely equity financed, and it has 20 shares outstanding, selling at a price of $50 per share. Thus, the company is correctly valued in the market: assets are worth $1,000, and the total market value of its shares is $1,000.

Now, company strategists suddenly announce a new investment project. If we invest $150 now in cost-saving equipment, this will generate additional cash flows of \$25 per year forever. If the appropriate discount rate for the new cash flows is also 10 percent, we can calculate the project's N.P.V. as $-150 + 25/.10 = \$100$. Since N.P.V. is positive, the project is worthwhile.

The company announces that it will issue new shares to finance the project. New shares will not necessarily sell for the initial \$50 per share price, however, because the announcement of the project may affect the share price. Let's say that the company issues n^* new shares at a price P^*. Whatever values n^* and P^* take on, the company wishes to raise \$150 from the share issue, so $n^*P^* = 150$.

Now let's look at the company after the new shares have been issued and the project has been adopted. On the asset side of the company's market value balance sheet, the sum of the discounted cash flows from the old and new assets is $100/.10 + 25/.10$. On the liability side, we have $20 + n^*$ shares, all selling at a price of P^*. The balance sheet must balance, which implies:

$$\frac{100}{.10} + \frac{25}{.10} = (20 + n^*)P^*$$

We know that $100/.10$ can be written as 20×50, or the original number of shares times the original share price. We also know that n^*P^*, the proceeds from the new stock issue, is \$150. Making these two substitutions,

$$20(50) + \frac{25}{.10} = 20(P^*) + 150$$

Or, rearranging algebraically,

$$-150 + \frac{25}{.10} = 20(P^* - 50)$$

The left-hand side of the equation can now be recognized as the N.P.V. of the new investment project, while the right-hand side is the change in wealth for the original shareholders. This implies

When money is scarce, man and beast are very much alike: upon the least alarm, some run like foxes; and others are as familiar and crusty as bears.

Thomas McCulloch, The Stepsure Letters

that shareholders at the time the project is announced experience an increase in wealth that is just equal to project N.P.V. Specifically, the share price, P^*, must rise to \$55, so the original shareholders gain $20 \times 5 = 100$, which is exactly equal to project N.P.V.

This example strengthens the rationale for making corporate investment decisions according to the net present value rule: If the company's objective is to increase shareholder wealth, accepting positive-N.P.V. projects is always consistent with this objective. However, the example is subject to the qualification that the stock market must be efficient. That is, investors must recognize the value of the proposed project so that shares are issued at a price, P^*, which fully reflects the new project's N.P.V.

KEY 6

See your risk as your shareholders see it

Shareholders evaluate an investment project by discounting its expected future cash flows at a discount rate reflecting project risk. However, to understand the stock market valuation of new projects, managers must see project risk as their shareholders do.

Shareholders generally hold portfolios of securities and other assets, so they will evaluate the risk of any given project in terms of its contribution to their overall portfolio risk. Shareholders will not look at the risk of a company's project in isolation from other portfolio risks that they bear. This is important, because shareholders can reduce their overall risk through portfolio diversification. Returns on different risky assets are imperfectly correlated, so when these assets are held in combination, some of their return fluctuations cancel one another out.

Any asset's total risk has two components. The first is unsystematic or diversifiable risk. This component is part of the asset's total return variability, but when the asset is combined in a portfolio with other assets, unsystematic risk has a negligible effect on the overall portfolio's return variability. We say, therefore, that this component of risk can be diversified away in portfolios.

The second risk component is systematic or undiversifiable risk. Although asset returns are imperfectly correlated, they are still positively correlated, on average, to some degree. This is attributable to common economic threads, such as the business cycle and the general health of the world economy, which tend to affect all securities returns to one extent or another. As a result, even diversified portfolios display overall risk that is related to these common factors. For a portfolio, we refer to systematic risk as the irreducible return variability that remains, even if the portfolio has been diversified both internationally and across asset classes. A diversified portfolio contains largely systematic risk, but little or no diversifiable risk. For an individual asset, systematic risk is the risk that the security would contribute to a diversified portfolio, and this is related to the asset's susceptibility to common economic factors. Individual assets contain both systematic and diversifiable risk, but when they are combined in a portfolio, the diversifiable component diminishes in importance.

Because investors can eliminate unsystematic risk through portfolio diversification, we would not expect the capital market to offer any premium return for bearing it. Instead, shareholders can expect compensation only for systematic risk, and thus they will evaluate new investment projects in terms of their systematic, but not their diversifiable, risk.

This distinction between systematic and unsystematic risk is important because managers and shareholders may have conflicting views of risk. Managers have a good deal of their human capital tied to their companies and may feel less diversified with respect to their own companies' fortunes than the typical shareholder. Thus, managers may place greater importance on diversifiable risk than the average shareholder. Managers, for example, may favor projects that diversify the company's businesses and smooth out its cash flow stream. Shareholders, by contrast, can achieve such diversification at least as easily in their own portfolios. Thus, it is a project's systematic risk, not its diversifiable risk, that affects the stock market's valuation of the company. The discussion of the next two Keys will offer suggestions for measuring the systematic risk of a project.

KEY 7

Know your cost of capital

The discount rate used in net present value analysis is also called the cost of capital. Investors value a company by discounting anticipated future cash flows at the rate of return they could expect to earn elsewhere on assets of similar risk. Thus, the cost of capital is an opportunity cost, or the return investors sacrifice by not investing elsewhere. Because investors would not advance funds for a project unless they could expect to earn at least their opportunity cost, we can also interpret the cost of capital as a minimum acceptable rate of return. Finally, because investors can earn higher returns in the market for bearing more risk, the cost of capital reflects compensation for risk-bearing.

Risk has several dimensions. As we saw in the discussion of Key 6, we can distinguish between systematic and unsystematic risk. Because investors can eliminate unsystematic risk by holding diversified portfolios, only systematic risk is relevant in measuring the cost of capital. We can also distin-

> Money is the symbol of nearly everything that is necessary for man's well-being and happiness... Money means freedom, independence, liberty.

Edward E. Beals, The Law of Financial Success

guish between business and financial risk. Business risk is inherent in the company's operations. It would be present even if the company were entirely equity-financed. If the company uses debt financing, however, it also introduces financial risk. Through debt financing, or leverage, a company magnifies return fluctuations to shareholders, thus adding an additional layer of financial risk. The cost of capital must therefore include compensation for both business and financial risk.

The cost of capital is usually measured as a weighted average of the costs of equity and debt. Thus, the weighted average cost of capital (W.A.C.C.) can be represented as:

$$\text{W.A.C.C.} = r_E(E/V) + r_D(1 - T)(D/V)$$

r_E is the cost of equity, or shareholders required rate of return.

r_D is the cost of debt, or bondholders' required rate of return.

E/V and D/V are the ratios of the market values of equity and debt to total company market value.

T is the corporate tax rate.

Measuring the cost of equity requires a model of the risk-return tradeoff available to shareholders in the market. For example, the widely used Capital Asset Pricing Model measures the cost of equity as:

$$r_E = r_f + \beta(r_m - r_f)$$

r_f is the risk-free rate of return (as measured, say, by a government bond yield).

r_m is the expected return on the overall market portfolio (as proxied by, say, the S.&P. 500).

ß is the "beta" coefficient, a measure of systematic risk.

Estimates of company betas can be obtained from investment analysis services, such as Standard & Poors or Value Line.

The beta coefficient reflects both a company's business and financial risk.

Suppose, for example, that the current yield on 20-year U.S. government bonds is 6 percent. Historically, the risk premium on the market portfolio ($r_m - r_f$) has been about 8 percent. For a company with an estimated beta of 1.25, therefore, the cost of equity would be about 16 percent.

The cost of debt is measured as the yield on bonds that a company would issue now to finance a project. This yield is multiplied by one minus the corporate tax rate, reflecting the fact that interest expense is tax deductible.

Suppose that the company whose beta is 1.25 undertakes a project. The financing proportions (measured at market value) will be 75 percent equity and 25 percent debt. The company could issue bonds today at a yield of 8 percent and the corporate tax rate is 35 percent. The weighted average cost of capital is then $.16(.75) + .08(.65)(.25) = .133$.

KEY 8

The cost of capital is project-specific

We can calculate W.A.C.C. for a company as a whole, as in the example in Key 6, but it is important to remember that the cost of capital is really a project characteristic. We can think of a project as a stand-alone company with a separate balance sheet and then ask how investors would value this company's securities. As with other companies, investors would discount expected project cash flows at a rate that reflects both its business and financial risk.

Investors would calibrate the required return for business risk to the returns available on other companies in similar businesses. They would also consider the debt and equity financing proportions that this type of project could support. In principle, then, each project has its own weighted average cost of capital. For an "average" project, such as expanded capacity for its principle product line, this may be the same as the overall company's cost of capital. However, for projects such as introducing an entirely new product, the required return may differ significantly from the company's overall W.A.C.C.

By evaluating projects alone, managers can avoid two common mistakes. The first arises when we apply the company's overall cost of capital to all projects. Like traded securities, projects tend to exhibit a tradeoff between risk and return. Higher risk projects tend to have higher returns and vice versa. The challenge for capital expenditure analysis, then, is to determine whether a project's expected return is high enough to compensate for its risk.

Suppose we have a list of possible projects, ranked from low to high risk. If this list is typical for the company, the overall W.A.C.C. should reflect the risk of the average project in the list. But then if we use the overall W.A.C.C. to discount each project's cash flows, the projects with below average risk and return will tend to have lower N.P.V.s, while high-risk, high-return projects will tend to have higher N.P.V.s. Thus, a company following the N.P.V. rule with a single cost of capital will be biased toward high-risk projects. This bias can be avoided if we assess the risk of each project separately and apply a cost of capital commensurate to that risk.

The second common mistake is attributing debt capacity to a project that really comes from the company as a whole. Because corporate interest payments are tax deductible, some amount of debt financing is generally believed to lower the cost of capital, at least up to the point where the risk of financial distress becomes unacceptable. Suppose a company that has no debt is evaluating a project. In view of the underleveraged capital structure, management decides it could finance the project entirely with debt, so sets the project's W.A.C.C. equal to the cost of debt.

The flaw in this reasoning is that the project could never support 100 percent debt on its own. Rather, management is drawing on unused debt capacity from the company's other assets in financing the project. However, the company could have supported more debt whether or not it adopted this project. Because the debt capacity is not project-specific, we bias the analysis toward acceptance by assuming 100 percent debt financing. The more accurate procedure would be to attribute an amount of debt to this project that it could support on its own.

> Being good in business is the most fascinating kind of art... Making money is art and working is art and good business is the best art.

Andy Warhol, From A to B and Back Again

KEY 9

Estimate incremental cash flow effects

When estimating a project's future cash flows, it is important to include all incremental effects. We must include all cash flows resulting from a current decision and exclude any cash flows that are unaffected by this decision.

Suppose we buy a new computer that we expect to last for three years. The cost of the computer is an obvious cash outflow, but we must also consider what we would have done had we not bought the computer. If we would have continued using an old computer, an additional result of buying the new computer is that we sell the old one now. We should therefore include in project cash flows the proceeds from the sale plus any associated tax consequences. Furthermore, had we not bought the new computer, we would have sold the old one at the end of three years. In buying the new computer, we forgo the proceeds from selling the old one in three years, and this should be included as a project outflow.

Other situations in which one project interacts with another require care in estimating incremental cash flows. Suppose we manufacture and distribute cola drinks and are considering development of a new diet cola. If some of the sales of our new product will come at the expense of existing ones, not all of the sales of the new product represent truly incremental cash flows. On the other hand, if competitors are highly likely to develop a diet cola, erosion of our existing product sales may occur whether we develop a diet product or not. In this case, the erosion is really not an incremental effect of our new product development.

Project opportunity costs should also be included. Suppose we develop the diet cola and then use an idle bottling line in one of our existing plants to bottle the new drink. If the capacity is truly idle, the use of this equipment does not cause any incremental capital expenditure. However, if sales of our other products are growing, and if our use of the idle capacity will cause us to build new bottling capacity sooner than we otherwise would, a capacity charge should be levied against the diet-cola project. Such charges can sometimes be estimated from rental rates. For example, if use of the idle bottling capacity causes us to build new capacity two years earlier than otherwise, we could charge two years worth of bottling line rental fees to the new project.

Of course, we should not charge a project with costs that are not truly incremental. We might be tempted to charge the diet cola project with part of the cost of heat and light in our bottling plant. However, if these overhead costs would have been the same without new product, they are not incremental to the diet cola project.

Finally, it is important to keep in mind that capital

expenditure decisions are always forward looking, so we should ignore sunk costs. If we have already incurred product-development and test-marketing costs and are deciding whether to proceed with production of our diet cola, the costs that have already been incurred are no longer relevant. That money has been spent, and it cannot be recovered if we do not go ahead with production, so it has no bearing on the production decision at this time.

KEY 10

Don't forget additional investment in working capital, plant and equipment

A project's operating cash flows include after-tax cash revenues and expenses as well as the tax effects of depreciation. While these are easily recognized as components of project cash flow, periodic changes in net working capital and capital expenditures, which can have equally important consequences, are often overlooked.

Net working capital is defined as current assets minus current liabilities. The primary current asset items include cash and marketable securities, accounts receivable and inventories, while current liabilities include accounts payable and any other accrued liabilities, such as taxes. The items comprising net working capital are sometimes referred to as spontaneous assets and liabilities. That is, they arise spontaneously in the normal course of doing business. To help product sales, a company needs to maintain a transaction balance in cash and marketable securities. Increased sales generally require increased inventories, and credit sales generate receivables. Similarly, an increased level of sales tends to increase accounts payable, accrued taxes and other accrued expenses.

The increased current assets needed to support sales are a use of funds, while the increased current liabilities are a source of funds. Thus, any increases in net working capital are part of the cash outflows associated with a project. Changes in net working capital generally follow the pattern of sales, and it is important to include them in project cash flows. Changes in the needed working capital balance are often estimated as a fraction of the change in forecast sales from one period to the next.

It may seem strange to include any increases in cash balances as a project outflow. However, the point is that these balances must be on hand, on average, to support project-related transactions. They are tied to the project, therefore, and are not available for use elsewhere in the company. In this sense, they represent outflows from the standpoint of the rest of the company.

Changes in working capital also help reconcile accrual accounting statements with the flow of cash. As discussed under Key 2, credit sales are recognized on the income statement before customers have paid in cash. Thus, designating any increased receivables as a cash outflow offsets sales that have been included as inflows even when they have not yet been collected. In a similar fashion, accounting expenses cover only goods that have actually been sold, but do not include additions to inventory, so we need to include increased inventories as part of cash outflows. To the extent that we have not yet paid for raw materials added to inventory, however, we have generated accounts payable, and increases in payables are thus part of project inflows.

Just as projects require periodic infusions of working capital to support sales, they often require additional investments in fixed assets as well. Machines must be overhauled or replaced periodically, plants and other buildings must be renovated and maintenance expenses must be incurred. The amounts of these expenditures and the times at which they are expected to occur should be included in any accurate capital expenditure analysis.

KEY 11

Don't forget terminal value (but don't overestimate it, either)

It is important to include a terminal value, or an estimated project value at the end of the analysis period, in net present value estimation. However, it is also important to avoid gross over-estimates of terminal value.

It is typical to forecast project cash flows over some time horizon, such as five years. While we may not feel confident in making explicit cash flow forecasts beyond a limited horizon, however, projects rarely come to an abrupt halt. There may be a primary production period, on which we focus our analysis, but production may continue at a reduced rate thereafter. Alternatively, we may be able to sell project assets at the end of the primary period. In either case, our analysis should include the project's value at the end of the horizon.

A number of techniques are available for estimating a terminal value. If we introduce a new line of automobiles, it might be sufficiently advanced in terms of design or styling that we will be able to earn superior profits relative to competitors for the next three years. After that, however, competitors will have caught up, so our new product line assets will come to be valued similar to the average assets in the automobile industry. Thus, we could estimate a terminal value for the new product line at the end of three years by applying an industry average valuation multiple. Common choices include an industry average price-earnings ratio, applied to the project's estimated horizon date earnings, or the ratio of market value to either book value or earnings before interest, taxes, depreciation and amortization.

Terminal value is also estimated using one of the perpetual annuity models discussed under Key 3. If a product's competitive advantage gradually erodes, forecast cash flows may decline to a "steady-state" level that we would be willing to treat as a perpetuity. Alternatively, we might decide that, after a period of above-normal growth, sales increases will decline to a steady rate of, say, 2 percent per year. The growing perpetuity model can also handle negative growth rates. If we forecast a cash flow of 100 for the year after the analysis horizon, with cash flows declining steadily at 5 percent per year after that, then with a 15 percent cost of capital, our terminal value is

$$100/(.15 - (-.05)) = 500.$$

Another approach to estimating a terminal value is to focus on liquidation. We may conclude, for example, that assets like cash and accounts receivable could be recovered at roughly their book value, while assets like inventory and plant and equipment might yield only a fraction of their book values.

While it is important not to ignore terminal value, it is equally important not to overestimate it. Suppose a project is expected to generate cash flows 90, 100 and 110 in the first three years. We assume that after Year 3, project cash flows will grow at a 10 percent rate for the foreseeable future (i.e., 121 in Year 4, 133.1 in Year 5, etc.). If the cost of capital is 15 percent, the terminal value is $121/(.15 - .10) = 2,420$. In this case, the assumed terminal value completely dominates the N.P.V. calculation. It is important to realize that 10 percent is an extraordinary growth rate to last forever, and that this is probably an unrealistically optimistic assumption.

KEY 12

Include project tax consequences

Another essential element in estimating project cash flows is to include all relevant tax consequences. These are particularly important at the beginning and end of a project. During the course of the project, depreciation and interest tax shields must be treated properly.

At the end of a project, there are tax consequences if assets are sold for other than their book value at that time. Under current U.S. tax law, any gains or losses from assets sold for other than their book value are taxed at the ordinary corporate income tax rate. Thus, the net salvage value, N, of an asset that is sold for a price SV when its book value is BV and the corporate tax rate is T is given by:

$$N = SV - (SV - BV)T$$

For example, if the corporate tax rate is 35 percent, and an asset is sold for $20 million at a time when its book value is $10 million, the net salvage value is $16.5 million. If the same asset is

Business must be profitable if it is to succeed, but the glory of business is to make it so successful that it may do things that are great chiefly because they ought to be done.

Charles Schwab

sold for $5 million, it generates a tax saving, and the salvage value from the equation above is $6.75 million.

At the beginning of a project, it is important to be alert for investment tax credits (I.T.C.). There is currently no I.T.C. in effect in the United States, but there has been in the past and could be again. Other countries may have a credit currently in effect. If there is a 10 percent I.T.C. currently in effect, a company can take 10 percent of the amount invested in a given year and deduct it from its tax bill.

During the course of a project, an important tax effect is the depreciation tax shield. If cash flows are calculated as discussed under Key 2, depreciation has been subtracted from revenue in calculating net income. Thus the full amount of depreciation must be added to reflect that this is a noncash charge. It is also algebraically equivalent to simply subtract operating expenses from revenues, calculate taxes on that amount and add back the depreciation tax shield. For example, suppose revenue in a given year is $100, cash operating expense is $60, depreciation is $20 and the corporate tax rate is 35 percent. Net operating cash flow is calculated as $(100 - 60 - 20)(1 - .65) + 20 = \$33$, or, equivalently, as $(100 - 60)(1 - .35) + .35(20) = \$33$.

If depreciation tax shields are included in net operating cash flow, it is natural to ask why interest tax shields are not. Because interest is tax deductible, it generates a tax shield in the same way that depreciation does. However, as discussed under Keys 2 and 7, a project's operating cash flows do not include any financing flows. Rather, a traditional N.P.V. analysis considers the cash flows to the entire project, as if it were valuing the asset side of a balance sheet. It does not explicitly consider how those cash flows are distributed between bondholders and shareholders. The share of operating cash flow that goes to bondholders is taken into account by the weight on debt in the weighted average cost of capital, and the tax deductibility of interest is incorporated by using the after-tax cost of debt. As a result, the taxes calculated as part of operating cash flows are not the taxes that the firm actually pays, but rather the hypothetical taxes that would be paid by an otherwise equivalent firm, financed entirely with equity. To the extent that the firm actually employs debt financing, these tax effects are incorporated in the weighted average cost of capital.

KEY 13

Inflation: be consistent between cash flows and discount rates

When inflation is expected to cause future changes in prices, it is important to distinguish between real and nominal cash flows and discount rates. Nominal cash flows are measured using the prices prevailing at the time the cash is received. Thus, inflation creates differences between real and nominal cash flows. Similarly, real discount rates are based on returns that are measured in constant price level, or constant purchasing power terms, while nominal rates are based on the dollar returns an investor actually receives.

The basic rule for capital budgeting in the face of inflation is to discount nominal cash flows at the nominal cost of capital or real cash flows at the real cost of capital. Either approach, correctly applied, will yield the same answer. Suppose, for example, that a project requires an initial investment of $100 and has real after-tax cash inflows of $30 per year for five years. If the real discount rate is 8 percent, project N.P.V. is:

$$N.P.V. = -100 + \frac{30}{1.08} + \frac{30}{(1.08)^2} + \frac{30}{(1.08)^3} + \frac{30}{(1.08)^4} + \frac{30}{(1.08)^5} = 19.78$$

If a 5 percent annual inflation rate is expected during the life of the project, and if all cash flow components are equally affected by inflation, then the nominal cash flows in Years 1, 2, ..., 5 are, respectively, $30(1.05)$, $30(1.05)^2$, ..., $30(1.05)^5$. Because investors will presumably be concerned with the purchasing power, rather than the dollar amount, of their returns, they will demand a nominal return, r_n, that compensates them for the rate of inflation, i. Thus, if 5 percent inflation is expected, and if the real required return is 8 percent per year, the nominal required return is given by:

$$(1 + r_n) = (1.08)(1.05)$$

This implies that the nominal rate of return is 13.4 percent. If we discount the nominal cash flows at the nominal discount, we obtain

$$N.P.V. = -100 + \frac{30(1.05)}{1.134} + \frac{30(1.05)^2}{(1.134)^2} + \frac{30(1.05)^3}{(1.134)^3} + \frac{30(1.05)^4}{(1.134)^4} + \frac{30(1.05)^5}{(1.134)^5} = 19.78$$

the same as we obtained discounting real cash flows at the real discount rate.

While the basic rule for treating inflation is relatively straightforward, it is also easy to make mistakes. One common mistake stems from not all cash flows being equally affected by inflation. In particular, depreciation is always given in nominal terms. When an asset is purchased, its initial book value is set forever, and the tax laws stipulate how many nominal dollars of depreciation expense may be deducted from taxable income during each year of the project's depreciable life. This is independent of what the inflation rate turns out to be during that time. If we are discounting nominal cash flows at the nominal discount rate, depreciation expense is unaffected by inflation. On the other hand, if we are discounting real cash flows at a real discount rate, depreciation expense must be deflated for each year's inflation. Because depreciation is fixed in nominal terms at the time an asset is purchased, it therefore declines in real terms in the face of inflation.

A second common mistake occurs when staff analysts find it easier to project future sales and expenses in terms of product units rather than dollar amounts. While there is nothing wrong with this, it is important to remember that, if we are using a nominal discount rate, unit prices and costs must be adjusted for expected inflation. Too often, analysts project unit sales and then discount future cash flows at a nominal discount rate, without adjusting unit prices and costs for inflation. This can result in a significant underestimate of project N.P.V.

KEY 14

Overseas investment: incorporating exchange rates

Multinational corporations have projects in different countries whose cash flows are denominated in different currencies. This raises the question of whether to discount these cash flows in terms of our domestic currency or in foreign currency units. As in the case of inflation, it is important to be consistent between cash flows and discount rates.

One approach is to translate all foreign cash flows into our company's domestic currency and to discount at a home currency discount rate. Suppose a U.S. company has a German project. The initial cost of the project is DM 105, and it is expected to generate a cash flow of DM 126 in one year. Suppose the exchange rate between marks and dollars is currently 1.75 DM/US$, and that we expect this rate to change to 1.8 DM/US$ by next year. Given these current and expected future exchange rates, we can simply translate all cash flows into US$. Thus the initial outlay is equivalent to $60 and the future cash flow is equivalent to $70. If the discount rate in US$ terms is 10 percent, we can calculate project N.P.V. as $70/1.1 − $60 = $3.64.

This approach immediately translates all cash flows into our primary currency, and we use our own domestic cost of capital, which we might be able to estimate with some precision. However, to employ this approach effectively, we must be adept at forecasting future exchange rates. This is a perilous business at best.

A second approach is to leave the cash flows denominated in marks, discount at a mark-denominated discount rate, and then translate the resulting present value into US$ at the current exchange rate. This has the advantage that we need not forecast any future exchange rates. However, it does necessitate that we estimate our cost of capital in foreign currency terms.

Which approach is best? If international capital markets are efficient, both approaches should yield the same result. Suppose currency traders have the same expectation about the DM/US$ exchange rate that we do. An investor in the U.S. could invest US$1 for one year and have US$1.10 by the end of the year. The same investor could first translate the same dollar into DM1.75, invest at the mark-denominated interest rate, rDM, and translate the resulting marks back into dollars at an expected exchange rate of 1/1.8 US$/DM. If the two transactions are to have the same expected return, it must be the case that $1.1 = 1.75(1 + r\text{DM})/1.8$, or $r\text{DM} = .1314$. If so, interest rates in the two countries are in equilibrium and we can use either rate.

If we use the 13.14 percent market-denominated interest rate to discount the first year's DM 126 million cash flow in our example, we obtain a present value of DM 111.366 million, from which we subtract the initial cost of DM 105 for an N.P.V. of DM 6.366. Translating this into dollars at the current exchange rate then gives us $3.64 million, the same as before.

If we can obtain a good set of foreign interest rates for different terms to maturity, the advantage of this second approach is that we can use the consensus expectations about exchange rate movements, which are built into the relationships between interest rates across countries. This may be preferable to constructing our own exchange rate forecasts.

KEY 15

Watch out for project options

Most investment projects carry implicit options. An option is the right, but not the obligation, to take a specific action on a future date. Options are prevalent in the capital markets. Call options on common stocks convey the right to buy a common stock at a specified price on or before a specified date. These options are now widely traded, as are options on bonds, currencies and commodities. The options implicit in capital investment projects are not publicly traded, and they are often hidden, but they can add great value to a project, so it is important to be alert for them.

Before a project is initiated, it has a postponement option. I can drill a new oil well today, or I can wait for more information about possible future oil prices and the likelihood that there is actually oil at my drilling location. Postponing a project is not always the best decision, but it is important to realize that any project competes with the same project initiated at a later date.

Once under way, most projects also have abandonment options. If I start to drill an oil well, I can stop drilling if prospects are dimming. Alternatively, once a well is operational, I can stop producing at any point if expected revenue over the next period appears insufficient to cover my variable production costs. If I do stop production, I have the option to start up again should the outlook become more favorable, but I also have the option to cap the well and sell my fixed assets.

These options are valuable because they allow a company to react as information arrives and uncertainty is resolved. Rather than being saddled indefinitely with a particular cash flow stream once a project has been initiated, a company has options to expand, contract, abandon, or otherwise modify the project as future prospects become clearer.

Unfortunately, options are not amenable to valuation with standard discounted cash flow techniques. The sudden changes in risk that occur as uncertainty is resolved make it impossible to specify a risk-adjusted discount rate with any precision. Although space does not permit a full discussion of the option valuation techniques that have been developed, one insight that has emerged is especially noteworthy. We tend to think of an increase in risk as being harmful to security prices, but with options the opposite is true. This is because an option's downside risk is limited by my right not to exercise it. If I have an option to buy a stock at a fixed price, my upside potential is unlimited. However, if the stock's market price goes continually downward, I don't suffer continual losses. Rather, I simply choose not to exercise the option.

This option valuation principle affords a different

perspective on the uncertainty surrounding investment projects. As long as I have options to cut my losses, greater uncertainty can actually create opportunities and enhance project value. In the example of the oil well, greater uncertainty about future oil prices can increase the value of an operating well, because if oil prices go up dramatically, I can take full advantage by producing to capacity. On the other hand, if oil prices go down, I have the option to halt production. It is easy to overlook a considerable portion of a project's true value if the analyst is not alert to the presence of such options.

KEY 16

Know how and when to make replacement investments

Any piece of equipment can be replaced at any time during its useful life. Managers must decide when is the best time to make this replacement and which type of replacement equipment to choose. While these decisions should be made according to the net present value principle, replacement investments have special features that are worth noting.

To start with a simple case, suppose we have a printing press, and we are considering replacing it with a new, higher-speed model. To simplify matters, suppose both the existing press and the new one will come to the end of their useful lives at the same time. We can then analyze the replacement project by calculating all cash flows associated with the new press and subtracting the cash flows that would have occurred had we continued using the old press.

The initial outlay for the replacement project is the cost of the new press minus the after-tax proceeds from selling the existing one. If the new and old presses do exactly the same work, we need not consider project revenues because these will be identical whether we replace or not, but operating costs might be different. If the new press is faster, it might result in lower labor costs, for example. In addition, the annual depreciation tax shields associated with the two presses might be different. Finally, at the end of the project, we receive any after-tax proceeds from selling the new press minus what we would have received from selling the old. If the net present value of these cash flow differences is positive, replacement is worthwhile.

However, there are additional issues to consider. Replacing the existing press now may be better than running it until the end of its useful life, but it may be better still to wait and replace it later. This may especially be the case if there is rapid technological change and cheaper presses with lower operating costs are likely to appear soon.

A second complication is that the new press might have a different useful life from the old one. In addition, we might have more than one possible choice of replacement equipment, and these, too, might have different useful lives. A convenient technique for handling this problem is to calculate the present value of all future cash flows associated with each of the choices. We can then calculate the annual payment on an annuity that has the same present value and lifetime as the equipment in question. Comparing annual annuity payments across the different possible presses is then equivalent to comparing the annual costs we would incur if we kept replacing each machine with a like model indefinitely.

This comparison raises the further issue of hidden

options. We might be considering two possible replacement presses, one with a shorter useful life than the other. If we are in the midst of rapid technological change, the shorter-lived press carries with it the option to switch to a newer, better press should one be developed. The future course of technology is, of course, very difficult to predict. Nevertheless, it is important to be aware of the potentially valuable option of switching technologies that may be inherent in shorter-lived equipment.

KEY 17

Understand the value of R.&D.

One of the most important investments for many companies is research and development. R.&D. spending is often an integral element of corporate strategy. Any market advantage a company gains is ultimately susceptible to competitive erosion, so companies must continually seek to reinvigorate their advantages. For a pharmaceuticals company, such as Merck, or a consumer products company, such as Gillette, it is necessary to spend considerable sums for R.&D. to sustain the steady flow of new products and product improvements that erect and maintain barriers to entry and build competitive advantage.

While its importance is recognized, R.&D. spending is difficult to evaluate. Rather than subjecting it to the typical capital expenditure analysis, many companies simply allocate a certain percentage of sales to R.&D. each year. Such policies may work from a pragmatic standpoint, but they offer little assistance in allocating R.&D. funds among competing uses.

The reason R.&D. spending is difficult to evaluate by traditional discounted cash flow methods is that it entails future decisions. A company does not simply spend money on R.&D. now and then reap future cash flow benefits. Rather, a company spends now, and, depending on the results, may spend more on that line of research, may develop and market a new product, or may abandon that line of inquiry altogether. The essential point is that R.&D. is an investment in learning, and future decisions will be based on whatever is learned. The final outcome from R.&D. results from following a path through a decision tree, but the precise path ultimately taken is impossible to predict with any precision at the time the R.&D. expense is incurred.

Because R.&D. is really a program entailing numerous future decisions, it is more amenable to an options approach than to the traditional discounted cash flow approach. One insight that emerges from this approach is that options are more valuable the riskier the underlying asset. Thus, it may be fruitful to allocate at least small amounts of money to learning about highly uncertain prospects. Such funds can be thought of as purchasing options to further develop future products. If initial results are promising, we can proceed further down the path toward product development, and the ultimate reward might be quite large. If initial results cast doubt on ultimate success, on the other hand, we can abandon the product without making a major commitment of funds. The ideal R.&D. projects are those that can deliver a lot information about a product's feasibility and potential market reception without needing large expenditures in advance. The larger commitments can be made once some of the uncertainty about the product's potential has been resolved.

It is especially important to remember the sunk cost fallacy with R.&D. If the information gained from research turns out to be negative, the company should not fall into the trap of proceeding anyhow, simply because it has already spent so much on R.&D. Research and development can be an excellent investment before the fact, because there is some likelihood of a large payoff. By the same token, R.&D. has value because it allows us to step away from unpromising situations before making a major commitment of money. Once the money has been spent on R.&D., however, it is gone, and is no longer relevant to the decision of whether to proceed further.

KEY 18

Know where positive N.P.V.s come from

Suppose we analyze a project to introduce a new blend of ground coffee and find that it has a positive net present value. This implies that we estimate that the project can earn a higher return than we could expect to earn in a competitive market. Before we dive headlong into starting the project, it is important that we first understand the source of this positive N.P.V.

An estimated positive N.P.V. implies that our project has some source of competitive advantage. This may stem from economies of scale, a visible and respected brand image, superior product quality, a better distribution network, or some other business advantage that our competitors cannot presently duplicate. Without such an advantage, we could hope to earn no more than a competitive rate of return, and our project would have a net present value of, at most, zero.

If we cannot identify and articulate the source of competitive advantage that gives our project a positive N.P.V., this may cast doubt on our N.P.V. estimate. In ground coffee and other markets, competition is a harsh fact of business life, and over time, competition tends to erode most sources of business advantage. Even if we begin with a head start, it is in our competitors' economic interest to try to catch up. They can try to imitate our new product, improve their manufacturing or distribution efficiency, cut the price of a substitute product, or otherwise challenge our ability to earn superior returns. An awareness of the power of competition can help us avoid overly optimistic N.P.V. forecasts in two ways.

First, it is a good habit to approach any positive N.P.V. estimate with skepticism and caution. We should ask ourselves why we think competitors have not already tried the project we are contemplating. It is entirely possible that we really do have some source of advantage over other companies, but if we can identify that source, it may give us more confidence about our N.P.V. estimate.

Second, we should try to forecast the response of competitors to our project and build that response into our own cash flow estimates. To do that, we need to understand who our current and potential competitors may be and how quickly they might react to the challenge our project poses. If we have a source of competitive advantage initially, we need to estimate how easy it would be for competitors to duplicate it. Even if we have a barrier to entry, such as patent protection, we need to have an idea of how easy it might be to develop substitute products and of the strategies we will follow to defend our patent. We need to know how we will adjust our marketing plan in the face of competitive incursions. Will we increase advertising expenditures? Will we be able to sustain a cut in prices? Can we develop variations on our product that will present competitors with a continually moving target?

The ultimate impact of many of these moves may be to cut our own profit margins and reduce our cash flow, but unfortunately, that is the almost inevitable outcome of competition. Thus, an N.P.V. analysis that shows steady or rising cash flows extending into the indefinite future and includes no provision for competitive erosion should be regarded with considerable skepticism.

KEY 19

Watch out for biased forecasts

I n large corporations, ideas for capital expenditure projects often come up to headquarters from the plant or division level. Project proposals may have to pass through several approval levels, depending on their size, and they must be accompanied by supporting analysis, including cash flow forecasts, an N.P.V. calculation and other summary information. By subjecting each major project to several layers of scrutiny and analysis, this process is intended to insure that only value-enhancing projects are approved. For the process to work properly, however, top management must be alert for potential biases in the supporting analysis.

The forecasts in project proposals are often overly optimistic. Revenue is often overstated and cost understated. In part, this may stem from the natural enthusiasm of plant and division managers for ideas generated in their own units. Managers understand that they are competing for resources with other company units, and they want to see their own units prevail.

A company's incentive structures can also exacerbate the incidence of forecast bias. If the amount of the compensation pool going to a given division is based on measures of size, such as revenues or assets, division managers will have an incentive to lobby for projects that increase their own division's size. If top management wants to promote adherence to the net present value principle, it needs to insure that company incentives are consistent with that principle.

Unfortunately, this can be difficult to achieve. The N.P.V. principle considers costs and benefits over a project's entire life, so it may take considerable time before we learn with any accuracy whether a particular project is living up to its forecasts. Some companies even alter their investment criteria to make it easier to spot tendencies toward forecast bias. If companies impose a maximum "payback period," or length of time required for project cash flows to recoup the initial investment, it is relatively easy to determine whether a given division manager's forecasts are systematically biased. However, reliance on such a payback criterion carries its own perverse incentives, such as favoring projects that generate quick, but relatively modest payoffs at the expense of projects that need a longer time to develop but that will generate strong cash flows well into the future.

Another way to combat forecast bias is to ration funds. That is, in addition to requiring approval of individual projects, headquarters can stipulate that a division's total capital budget may not exceed a specified limit in any year. While this can limit spending on projects that have been justified by overly optimistic forecasts, budget limits that are too stringent also run the risk of screening out projects that really do have positive N.P.V.s.

Finally, top management can limit forecast bias by imposing centralized forecasts for variables that are not specific to a business unit. If a company has several divisions making different types of homebuilding materials, it may want to have all division managers base their revenue estimates on the same forecast of housing starts or population growth in the local area. It also may be advantageous to use company-wide forecasts of such variables as the level of inflation or the price of particular commodities, such as oil or copper.

To have enough is good luck, to have more than enough is harmful. This is true of all things, but especially of money.

Chuang-Tse

KEY 20

Perform sensitivity analysis

Once you have estimated a project's N.P.V., it is critical to understand your estimate's sensitivity to underlying assumptions. Your estimate depends on assumptions about product prices, operating costs, the cost of capital, working capital and capital expenditure requirements and terminal value. While all of these may be subject to bias or other forms of error, the final N.P.V. estimate may be more sensitive to some assumptions than others. It is important to identify which assumptions these are, so that we can devote special effort to assessing our faith in them.

Sensitivity analysis can be conducted in a variety of ways. First, we can simply change the assumed values for different variables, one by one, to gauge their impact. N.P.V. may turn out to be especially sensitive to the assumed product price or the gross margin, for example. If so, we need to consider the likelihood of business scenarios in which these variables would fall significantly below their assumed values. Estimates of a project's terminal value are often imprecise, so we need to be especially careful in examining projects with rapidly growing cash flows, in which the terminal value can dominate the N.P.V. calculation.

A project's estimated cost of capital can also be subject to considerable error. For short-lived projects, with most of the cash flow in the earliest years, moderate changes in the cost of capital may not affect N.P.V. very much. For long-lived projects with cash flows concentrated in the most distant years, on the other hand, project N.P.V. can be quite sensitive to the cost of capital estimate.

A second way to conduct sensitivity analysis is to find minimum or maximum values for certain variables for which project N.P.V. is still positive. Thus, we could find the minimum product price or the maximum operating cost per dollar of sales such that a project is still barely worthwhile. Spreadsheet features, such as "Solver" and "Goal Seek" in Microsoft Excel, can be quite useful in finding these minimum and maximum values.

Sometimes it is easier to rule out certain extreme values for a variable than it is to estimate its precise value. For example, an analyst may be unsure of just what product price a company will ultimately be able to charge, but at the same time sure that the price will not fall below $10 per unit. If project N.P.V. is still positive at a unit price of $10, we can have some confidence that N.P.V. is at least likely to be positive.

A more elaborate form of sensitivity analysis is simulation. This allows us to assign probability distributions to the variables that determine project N.P.V. and then simulate possible outcomes by taking random draws from the distributions. Software available as spreadsheet add-ins can carry out the calculations relatively quickly. The advantage of this technique is that it allows us to change all of the underlying variables simultaneously to get some idea of the range of uncertainty surrounding the ultimate N.P.V. outcome. Although simulation models can quickly become formidably complex, companies like Merck use them extensively to evaluate prospective research and development expenditures.

KEY 21

Continue to monitor projects after approval

Approval of a positive N.P.V. project does not signal the end of its analysis. Projects evolve as uncertainty is resolved, and company management continually faces additional decisions. By monitoring a project's progress, management can also gain valuable information that can be used to make better decisions about future projects.

The process of monitoring a project and checking actual results against forecasts is called project control and post audit. One purpose of this process is to insure that project options are continually analyzed. Every project carries an abandonment option that can be exercised at any point. At a given time, all funds previously spent are now sunk and no longer relevant to the decision of whether to continue the project. Thus, at each point, we need to assess whether future benefits that we can reasonably foresee from our current vantage point are sufficient to justify the expenditures we must still make. Projects are

Except during the nine months before he draws his first breath, no man manages his affairs as well as a tree does.

Bernard Shaw, **Maxims for Revolutionists**

often plagued by cost overruns, and, too often, management feels that, once the project has been approved, a commitment has been made to spend whatever it takes to get the project up and running. A good project control process can help avoid ill-advised expenditures by continuing to analyze the N.P.V.s of these additional investments.

Project post audit can also provide information about the analysts whose cash flow forecasts were used to justify the project in the first place. If we can identify sources of consistent bias in cash flow forecasts, we can adjust the forecasts made for future projects accordingly. In addition, the knowledge that today's forecasts will be checked against future results may temper an analyst's tendency to make overoptimistic forecasts.

However, two problems can limit the effectiveness of the post audit process. First, it can take a long time to get a clear picture of original forecast accuracy for a long-lived project. One or two years' results, even if they differ significantly from the original forecasts, may not be sufficient to conclude that the overall N.P.V. analysis was flawed.

Second, it can be very difficult after the fact to distinguish between bad decisions and bad luck. An N.P.V. analysis is inherently forward-looking. At a given time, the analyst projects future cash flows as well as they can be predicted at that point. One or two years later, we may have gained new information that invalidates the original forecasts. In natural resource extraction industries, a competitor may stumble on a new, easily mined deposit that suddenly shifts our own operation from low-cost producer to high-cost producer overnight. However, while that is an unlucky development, it does not mean that our original analysis was biased, or that the decision to develop our own extraction facilities was a bad one. It is the nature of uncertainty that new information, impossible to foresee, can turn what was prospectively a good decision into a bad one in hindsight. Conversely, a bad decision can wind up being bailed out by a lucky outcome.

Despite its limitations, most large companies carry out some form of project control and post audit for their capital expenditure programs. At the very least, this process forces management to continually reassess each project as events unfold.

KEY 22

Arrange financing with an eye toward future investment opportunities

In large part, the analysis of investment projects is conducted independently of financing decisions. The rationale is that, if a project has a positive N.P.V., we should be able to find a way to finance it. But in some instances, investment and financing decisions interact, and it is neither feasible nor prudent to try to keep them separate.

An important example is the relationship between current debt financing and future investment opportunities. Suppose that our manufacturing company has recently gone through a leveraged buyout and that 80 percent of our capital structure consists of debt. The debt carries a high coupon rate to compensate bondholders for the risk of default, which is not negligible.

Now suppose that a new investment opportunity arises unexpectedly. Because of a sudden technological advance, we can install new, high-speed assembly equipment on our production line. Over time, this equipment will increase product quality and reduce unit production costs significantly. Unfortunately, because of our already high leverage, our debt agreements restrict us from issuing additional debt. Our bondholders already face significant default risk, and they do not want to share the available asset pool with new creditors should we default.

This leaves us to finance the new project with equity, from either retained earnings or a new stock issue. If we do, however, our existing bondholders will experience a windfall gain. The new project increases company value, and some of this increase will go to the bondholders. Not only does the added profitability stemming from the new machinery reduce the probability of default, but bondholders also have a claim on the new assets as well as the old ones in the event we do default. As a result, our outstanding bonds will increase in value.

Because bondholders capture some of the value of the new investment project, the entire N.P.V. does not go to our shareholders. In fact, if bondholders gain enough, the N.P.V. to shareholders alone can be negative. That is, the gain to shareholders as a result of undertaking the project may be less than the amount of funds shareholders must advance to undertake it. In such cases, the shareholders have no incentive to undertake the project, even though it has a positive N.P.V.

The upshot is that companies must plan their current capital structure with an eye toward future investment needs. Large amounts of debt financing are imprudent for companies that are likely to have substantial investment opportunities. For such companies, bondholder gains from new projects can weaken or even eliminate incentives to undertake the projects in the first place. Thus, a company that spends substantial amounts on R.&D. should not be issuing a lot of debt, because the R.&D. is likely to generate new investment opportunities. A further implication is that companies with future investment opportunities should try to maintain some financial slack. This could be in the form of cash or unused debt capacity that could be called upon when favorable new investments arise. A company that still has the ability to issue debt or to draw down cash is less likely to see its future investment opportunities held hostage by already-outstanding debt issues.

If you want one year of

prosperity, grow grain.

If you want ten years of

prosperity, grow trees.

If you want one hundred

years of prosperity,

grow people.

Chinese Proverb

KEY 23

Be alert for project-specific financing opportunities

A project's characteristics may result in financing opportunities that can enhance N.P.V. In some cases, this takes the form of financing subsidies, such as low-interest loans or loan guarantees that a host government offers to attract investment. In other cases, the project's attributes may allow it to be effectively separated from the rest of the company and financed in a way that minimizes negative interactions with the company's capital structure.

We saw in Key 22 that a company with significant debt could forgo even an investment with a positive N.P.V. This is because, if the project were undertaken, a portion of the benefit would go to the company's existing bondholders rather than the shareholders. However, if the company's existing debt agreements allow it to issue additional senior debt, either secured debt or project financing may enable it to mitigate this problem. With both forms of financing, the new lenders have a prior claim on the project. In the case of secured debt, this claim is on the new project's assets, and because that gives existing bond-holders only a junior claim on the same assets in the event of bankruptcy, they benefit much less from its adoption. In the case of project financing, as with an oil pipeline, the new lenders have a prior claim on the pipeline's cash flows. In either case, the company can negotiate financing terms for the new debt that fully incorporate the value of the new project, so shareholders can capture the entire N.P.V.

Another means of separating a project from the rest of the company is leasing. If a company leases assets, such as rail cars or jet aircraft, ownership of the asset remains with the lessor, and the lessor can claim the asset in the event of default, thus reducing the amount of project benefits that go to existing bondholders. Leasing can also carry other benefits. If the company agrees to an operating lease (usually for a term shorter than the asset's useful life), it has the option, often prior to the expiration of the lease, to switch to newer equip-ment. This can be especially valuable with assets subject to technical obsolescence, such as com-puter equipment. In addition, leasing can be valu-able for companies that are not in a taxpaying position, so that such tax benefits of ownership as depreciation and interest tax shields would other-wise go to waste. Through leasing, a company can pass these benefits on to a taxable lessor and then negotiate a lease payment that reflects the value of these tax benefits to the lessor.

A final form of project-specific financing is a lim-ited partnership. Biotechnology companies have used these to pay for specific R.&D. projects for new pharmaceuticals. If a new drug succeeds, the partnership shares are typically bought out by the parent company, which then proceeds with further development and marketing. If the drug fails, shareholders of the parent company are partially insulated because the project is the responsibility of the partnership investors, rather than the parent company. Such arrangements can also allow better investor scrutiny of projects. If the company as a whole conducts a portfolio of R.&D. projects, it is difficult to accurately gauge the progress of any one of them. The partnership structure, on the other hand, may appeal to investors who would like to invest in and monitor one specific new product.

KEY 24

Mergers: understand incremental benefits

I n principle, evaluating a proposed merger with another company is no different from any other capital expenditure project. We need to estimate the incremental merger cash flows, discount these at an appropriate rate, and subtract the merger's cost. If N.P.V. is positive, the merger is worthwhile.

A common approach to estimating incremental merger benefits is to value the combined firm and then subtract the sum of the pre-merger market values of the separate companies. Given this incremental merger benefit, the cost is the premium that the acquiring company pays over the pre-merger market value of the target. We can then calculate N.P.V. as the difference between incremental benefit and cost.

While there is nothing wrong with this approach to merger evaluation in principle, it does run the risk of overestimating merger benefit by overestimating the value of the combined company. It is

> **The great way to inspire**
>
> **brotherly love all round**
>
> **is to keep on getting**
>
> **richer and richer till you**
>
> **have so much money**
>
> **that everyone loves you.**

Stephen Leacock, Further Foolishness

all too easy to become overly enthusiastic about the combined company's prospects and to project indefensibly high combined future cash flows. When a low-risk company acquires a higher-risk company it is also easy to apply the lower-risk company's cost of capital to the combined company's cash flows and overestimate the merged company's value.

A possible antidote to these problems is to start with the acquired company's pre-merger market value and then add the value of identifiable merger benefits. It is important to measure the target's market value prior to any speculation about a possible merger. If we measure market value after investors have already anticipated a merger, the company's value will already reflect anticipated merger benefits, as well as the estimated probability that the merger will be successful. If we measure market value prior to any merger speculation, on the other hand, this will reflect only investors' valuation of the company given the business policies put in place by current management. The incremental benefit of the merger, then, is the value of any policy changes that the acquiring management can achieve. The cost of the merger is still the premium paid by the acquirer.

Estimating merger N.P.V. with this incremental value approach has the benefit that it forces the acquiring management to identify the sources and the size of any operating improvements from the merger. It is easy to overestimate the total cash flows from the combined company, because we have no benchmark for comparison purposes. With the incremental value approach, on the other hand, pre-merger market value serves as the benchmark. If we have a good idea of the expected cash flows that are reflected in that value, then we must identify the operating improvements we hope to achieve.

Focusing on incremental benefits can also force management to assess how easily and how soon such benefits can be achieved. In some of the large mergers in commercial banking, oil and telecommunications, estimated benefits typically include substantial cost savings from the elimination of duplicate facilities and staff. However, management must also make good estimates of how long it will take to realize such benefits and what stumbling blocks may lie in the way, such as defections of key staff members. The incremental value approach to calculating merger N.P.V. can help focus management attention on these issues.

KEY 25

Mergers for stock: know how much you are paying

Wh
en one company acquires another, it can pay cash or stock. In a cash deal, the acquiring company buys all of the target company's common shares for cash. In a stock deal, the acquiring company issues new shares and exchanges them for the target company's shares. In the latter case, the target company's former shareholders become shareholders in the combined company.

The calculation of the merger N.P.V. is conceptually straightforward in a cash deal. If Company A buys Company B, the gain, or "synergy," from the acquisition is equal to the market value of the combined company minus the sum of their pre-merger market values. The acquisition's cost is the amount paid in cash for Company B minus the previous market value of B. This represents the amount of the merger gain that is shared with B's original shareholders. The net present value is the difference between the gain and cost. Suppose, for example, that A and B each have a total market value of $100 million prior to any merger announcement. If the combined company is worth $250 million, the merger has produced a gain in value of $50 million. If A agrees to pay $115 million in cash to acquire B, the merger's cost is $115 − $100 = $15 million, and the N.P.V. is $50 million − $15 million = $35 million.

When the merging companies exchange shares, on the other hand, the acquiring company gives an ownership share in the combined company to the target company's shareholders. The acquisition's true cost thus depends on the combined company's market value. Suppose that the same two companies from our previous example merge for stock. Specifically, let each company have 1 million shares outstanding originally and let A exchange one A share for each B share currently outstanding. Because the companies exchange shares in a one-to-one ratio, the former B shareholders wind up with a 50 percent ownership share in the combined company. Because half the combined company is worth $125 million, the merger's cost in the case of the share exchange is $125 million − $100 million = $25 million, so the merger's N.P.V. is $50 million − $25 million = $25 million. Under the terms described here, A's shareholders have given a bigger piece of the merger gain to B's shareholders in the share exchange deal than in the cash deal.

However, if the combined company turns out to be worth less than originally expected, the cost of the stock deal adjusts, whereas that of the cash deal does not. If the combined company turns out to be worth only $210 million, the gain falls to $10 million. The cost of the cash deal is still $15 million, so the deal will now be seen in retrospect to have been bad for A's shareholders. In the stock deal, on the other hand, the value of a 50 percent ownership share is now only $105 million, so the merger has cost only $5 million, and the merger N.P.V. is still $10 million – $5 million = $5 million.

The essential point in these examples is that a merger's N.P.V. depends on the value of the consideration paid to the acquired company. If payment is in cash, the value of the consideration is fixed. If payment is in stock, the value of the consideration depends on the market value of the combined company.

Let him look to his bond.

Shakespeare, The Merchant of Venice

INDEX

AUTHOR

ROBERT A. TAGGART, Ph.D. is Professor of Finance at Boston College's Wallace E. Carroll School of Management. He has previously held faculty appointments at Boston University and Northwestern University. He served as Editor of *Financial Management* from 1984 to 1987 and as President of the Financial Management Association in 1989–90. He is currently Corporate Finance Editor of the *Journal of Economics and Business*. He is author of *Quantitative Analysis for Investment Management*, as well as numerous articles in finance and economics journals.